Persian Pony

PERSIAN PONY

MICHAEL MCCLURE

Ekstasis Editions
Ekstasis Editions America

Copyright © Michael McClure 2017
Cover art & design: Amy Evans McClure
Author photo: Garrett Caples

U.S. edition published in 2018 by:

Ekstasis Editions America
840 Apollo St., Suite 100
El Segundo, California 90245
USA

Canadian distribution by :

Ekstasis Editions Canada Ltd.
2808 Prior St.
Victoria, BC V8T 3Y3
Canada

"Red Cages" and "Boulder Hill" were published as a chapbook by Blue Beetle Press in 1992.

All rights reserved. No part of this book may be reproduced in any form without the written permission of the publisher, with the exception of brief passages in reviews. Any request for photocopying or other reproduction of any part of this book should be directed in writing to the publisher or to ACCESS: The Canadian Copyright Licensing Agency, One Yonge Street, Suite 800, Toronto, Ontario, Canada, M5E 1E5.

Visit Ekstasis Editions online at www.ekstasiseditions.com to view our current catalog.

LIBRARY OF CONGRESS CATALOGING-IN-PUBLICATION DATA

CIP DATA may be obtained from the Library of Congress.

ISBN hardcover: 978-1-7324458-4-0
ISBN paperback: 978-1-7324458-3-3

"A thousand Persian ponies fell asleep in the moonlit plaza of your forehead, while through four nights I embraced your waist, enemy of the snow..."

—Frederico García Lorca

CONTENTS

Author's preface	11
Introduction by Paul E Nelson	13
The Soft New Soul	17
The Lute of Narcissus	19
Ivory Statuette	31
Morning Song for Big Sterl	35
To Seth Bunnel	36
Spontaneous Poem, Morning After Reading *When I Was a Poet*	37
Joanne Kyger	39
Blake Flakes	40
Plumed Stones	41
Peep	42
Dream Deep	43
High	44
Thrice Blessed	45
Shakespeare's Rose	46
Forgiveness Please	48
The Francesco Clemente Poem	50
Go Out	51
Quantum	52
Evidence	53
Everpresent	55
Twitter-In-Chief	57
A Climb	58
For Stefano Scodanibbio	59
Alive as Cupids	61
Smoke in a Hailstorm	63
Hoodoo	64
Rain on Orange	65
The Rainy Deck	66

Thalassaa	67
The Ashraf Fayahd Poem	68
Antelope Breath	70
Nitrous Oxide High	71
Spreading Petals	73
Light Light Light	75
November Valentine	77
Details	79
Fa T'sang	80
Tiny Nails	81
No Savior	82
December Semaphore	83
Venice Beach, At Last	84
Lungomare	85
Greeting	86
Mesembryanthemums	87
For Amy	88
Wrinkles and Scars	89
Wharf Pilings	90
Skeleton Key	91
Late Winter	92
With Simone Fattal at the Hockney Show	93
Yes	94
Joko Dave Haselwood	95
Spirit Neurons	96
Dying is Nothingness	98
The Mask of Grammar	99
Essay on the Media	100
Red Cages	103
Boulder Hill	112

ONCE THIS WAS ALL BLACK PLASMA & IMAGINATION

This book is for

THE PROTECTION OF ALL BEINGS

WITH DEEP HEART'S LOVE FOR

AMY   JAMES   JANE   BILL   MICHAEL

*** *** ***

"A mouse is miracle enough
to stagger sextillions of infidels."
— Walt Whitman

AUTHOR'S PREFACE

Poems in *Persian Pony* are written in PROJECTIVE VERSE, a mode conceived by Charles Olson. Projective Verse is neither metrical nor free verse. It gives swift access to the energy of inspiration moving to the Heart where it bounces through the syllable to the Breath and onto the field of composition. The field of composition may be paper or a screen or a listener's consciousness. This mode may or may not be beautiful, but it is not effortless. It has a commonality with the work of Jackson Pollock and Clyfford Still. In these poems capitals do not need to be spoken loudly. "The flow of energy through the system acts to organize the system," wrote Harold Morowitz.

Single letter lines moving down the page move normally as breath does. Poetry is a muscular principle. POETRY MUST BE REAL AS SWIRLS IN TAR ON THE STREET AND ROSES THAT HANG ABOVE THEM.

<pre>
               EAGLES
                seen
               on acid
                are
                 h
                 o
                 r
                 s
                 e
                 s

            IN CLOUDS.
</pre>

EXPERIENCES

are

nanoscale

and
vast

as
the disappearing

Anthropocene.

These poems wish to be art and nature and free to time-dive like Orcas in Cascadian waves.

Romantic Philosopher Friedrich Schlegel wrote: "All art should become science and all science art; poetry and philosophy should be made one."

Praise to my gifted friends who have brought me these awarenesses.

And praise and love to my wife, beloved Amy — always . . .

INTRODUCTION

Out less than a year after his last book *Mephistos,* poet Michael McClure gives us the radical vision that he's utilized for over sixty years as a poet, playwright, novelist and essayist. *Persian Pony* is a summing up of all he stands for since he began writing projective verse in the early 1950s. This latest work from a world-class athlete of openness reflects an oeuvre filled with curiosity, love, and deep experience—an interconnected vision.

With the dedication, FOR THE PROTECTION OF ALL BEINGS, McClure reiterates the title of a journal he co-edited in the early 60s that was part anarchism, part Buddhism, and a strike against censorship. His environmental awareness was taking shape in the 50s, when he gave his first reading at the Six Gallery in 1955.

In an early poem, "Action Philosophy" McClure displayed his "mammal patriotism" by writing that to prevent himself from being shaped as anything "less than spirit," he could choose to be "an otter / sailing on the silver water / beneath the rosy sky." Otter returns here in the core poem "The Lute of Narcissus" as Lutra, and depicted as "twin sister" swimming "beneath the surface" of their pool. The Otter has been a creature with significant personal mythological import for McClure.

McClure's poetic courage plumbs the depths of perception, achieves a precision of luminous details, a striking originality, and a range of expression from the cosmic to the microscopic. The results are stunning, humorous and liberating, and these come in rapid succession. Readers of this book have a wisdom harvest ahead of them. With McClure these moments arrive over and over in lines like:

> LET OUR LIVES FALL APART LIKE A TRUE POEM

and

> I AM WHAT I HAVE THE NERVE TO BE
> A HUGE SUCCESS
> HIDING IN MEAT.
> MAMMAL SHIVERING IN RAIN.

and

Everything of us is the Messiah.

    This is a reflection of interconnectedness (a tenet of Hua-yen Buddhism) embodied, and McClure's work is an experience of the authenticity of that interdependent origin of the universe. That mammal patriotism. What it IS rather than what it is *like*. A fathom deeper, directness and concision is part of the high-energy construct that the poem becomes in McClure's hands.

Paul E. Nelson
Rainier, Washington

Persian Pony

THE SOFT NEW SOUL

THE SOFT NEW SOUL
with its capsule of masks,
tender and quivering
ascends into matter
and here I am
breathing the old air
the ancient breath
of star formation
EVERYTHING
is past understanding
without inspiration
and fearlessness.
It's a small white dog on a leash
mindlessly waiting
In the wreckage of suicide wars.
Like used tee shirts and munitions
the surface of this strata
also covers itself in concrete
bridges and airports.
but
we
know
that,
and our pulse speeds
in the psychosis
yearning to be free
AND

THIS

THIS

THIS!

is freedom
and liberation.

THE LUTE OF NARCISSUS:
RECEIVING THE COMMISSION

I

REST
HERE

in active gentle thought
SOMETIMES MUSCLES ARE GENTLE SLEEPING THINGS
My eyes seek Lutra

Lutra twin sister

SHE SWIMS BENEATH THE SURFACE

of the pool

LUTRA,

GLORIOUS
LUTRA,

rise up

TIRESIAS is hobbling
this way

that old fuck,

he swings both ways,

served seven years as a temple whore

after he beat up the coupling snakes

and blind, too.

He, told my Mama Liriope

I would have a long life   IF

I never recognize my self.

    May Papa Cephissus
        wash that creaky bat
   away
  in the
    River

oooooops!

NASTY ECHO
and her sister nymphs
    (all of them copycats)

cry from the woodsy cliffs:
. . . love me
. . . love me
. . . love me . . .

Righteous JUNO in
her Olympianity

scoffs at them

∾

What they heard is,
You
cannot
love
me,
now
(endlesssly
they
echo
back

∾

A warm and sunny day here
                        lying on my bank
              with smiling flowers,
   only missing are the deep
                            bluepools of
                                    Lutra's eyes

Lutra, Sister Lutra, twin,
            come up   come out
   where deer friends
                  bend dappled necks
    to drink
           at the cushy marge

     water striders move slow here
                             and dart
   with feet in dots of light

                    ∾

          SOMETIMES
           by firelight

        we
        EAT
            the deer

          — taken from my
                    NETS

॒

      THE HIGH
           SKY
   today

     IS CLEAR
except for five battling
    SNAKE and EAGLE
    COUPLES

they never give it up

          — all day long

    ONE EAGLE

    ONE SNAKE

   make a pair.

  Plumed serpent heads
strike with splashing VENOM
     into feathered bird thighs
    and muscled chests

BLUE AND WHITE POWER PINIONS
  RAISE UP SCALED FEET
     with knotty talons
to tear
   writhing copper into red

Shining necks
> TWINE TWIST WRITHE
> in
> sweating air

    coil in coil

WINGS SNAP AND FLARE
> sparks
> flashing.

Joined COUPLES PLUMMET
> dropping toward
> the many-
> voice'd sea

HISS   SCREAM

WINGS BEATING

    plummeting

Then go
> STRATOSPHERIC

and
CRASH
> to the breaker tips

   Rise again
   then again

   until night

       They reappear in the Dawn.

•

     That's it.

༄

I
LOOK TO THE CALM
   brown-silver
        pool
My dark
   eyebrows
are handsome
       Tan cheeks
        are ruddy

   What large eyes
   and shapely cheekbones!

༄

"NARCISSUS, OH BROTHER
NARCISSUS . . . "

Lutra's upward face

      B
      R
      E
      A
      K
      S
our pool.

Sunstruck light
  is dimmer
in her presence.
        Blue eyes irradiate
the day.

"Narcissus clasp me in
      your muscled arms.
  My temple is
     your solid
          shoulder."

My dark eyes smile
back
to
Lutra!

   Oftentimes
   she dives
     deep and long
    beneath our lotus margined home
   through liquid corridors
   into the Black Light World.
     Where she speaks with
     Osiris-Green-Skin
   in his stygian cavern beneath
      deep caves

    where tormented Isis' lament
     soft and loud, soft and loud,
    is the only sound
      to hear.

     ∽

TIRESIAS HERE AGAIN!!

 His trudging cane
 thumps the ground . . .

Hey get out of here!
     GET OUT
OLD MAN

"Hrrrgg!" He responds, "Youth of ill star,
   dread fated one
     HEAR ME!
List' List' to me
 I come with orders.
     Commands for you both!
You shall obey this commission before
    you recognize
     your wearisome self!
 Otherwise you'll be
    skinned alive,
   turned inside out
   Flayed like impudent
       Marsyas"

"Old man," I shout,
 "Low born, no account , your mother is
     a minor nymph
   and your father — a shepherd.

  Go back to Papa and learn
   to play
     reed flute for goats.

   On top of all, you're
    wrinkled as
    a tortoise leg!"

"I assert to you," speaks Lutra,

"by this pool I dive in,

no disrespect dyes Narcissus' words . . . "

   Crude Tiresias sez:
  "Both of you Twerps
                must list' to commands
                     I bear . . . "

Narcissus:
 "Do you still try to augur
          by asking
                    those who can see
          about the flights
                of birds?
             Lay off!
         Get out!"

Tiresias sez:
 "Don't flex those lovely arms at me!!
      Both of you have
               been chosen . . . "

  "Chosen — by who?"

  "By you know 'WHO!'"

  "To do What?" I say

"To rescue Good Prince Peter Kropotkin

nabbed by hordes of ice giants
as he explored Sijberia . . . "

•

— to be continued —

IVORY STATUETTE
for Sterling Bunnel

    LIKE THIS . . . I PLACE THE IVORY STATUETTE
of reality
UPON
ITS
GOLDEN
BASE

IT
IS STERLING'S

HOWL
OF
PAIN

HIS CRY
OF
MOMENTARY
agony

then he sleeps
and
WAKES

ROARING LAUGHTER

tells
us

his visionary dream
invented colors
of a daughter becoming mosquito goddess.

Boasts of the size of his turds,

tells of the Oversoul

how the democratic hierarchies
of the spirit achieve themselves.

THIS SUPERHUMANLY ROBUST
and lifelong-powerful being
who has (really) escaped pursuing
water buffalo in the field
and staggered through

chest-deep stagnant mud
to collect the green-winged teal
brought down by his gyrfalcon. He will eat it
plucked and seared and running blood
with jalapeno jelly.

THIS MAN IS UNDOMESTICATED
he is the model of wolf before
becoming dog.
The huge deep mind of Cro-Magnon.

GREAT SKULL AND NO IMAGINED FEAR
but unending momentary ones.

MEMORY PERFECT
envisioning surface of stones
in the lightning-storm night of Oaxacan mountains
as he drives in rain-crumbling mud tracks
to bring back sacred mushrooms
and psychedelic salvia for research.
A YOUTHFUL TRIP.

YOU
ARE
O
R
I
G
I
NATOR
of our understanding
as we stand
open mouthed
hearing and seeing a landscape
before us in the Central Valley
as you open it
from the empty Praying Mantis egg case
on the gas station wall
to the swooping Redtail above.
Webs of life we have not seen
ARE
RIGHT
THERE.
And the illuminations in Kenya
and Iceland where we stand in awe of the Gyrfalcons
nesting, and the dead marauding Raven
on the moraine below.

Your robust energy and bodily power
is a force of nature
like the mind of Shakespeare.
You happen in front of us.

NOW YOU, LIKE ME,
ARE EXTREMELY OLD
and you are alive in this
shape
as I am.

YOU WISH TO BE FULLY ALIVE
to feel the actual passing
when that passage happens
fully conscious

AND
YOU
ARE.

And you will be
more and more

MORNING SONG FOR BIG STERL AFTER THE OPERATION

OVER THE HILLS IS OKEY-DOKE
the Moon is strawberry pie
Away, away the Furies fly
— AND FAIRIES COME OUT
to dance in the sky

The lizards swallow the scorpions down
and it's good eats for all,
the grubs a-smile in the carrion,
—VENISON
steams in the hall

Good cheer, Good cheer
the morn's a-riz,
soon you will view the clouds.
The pickled duck
marches towards noon

and
we shall frolic eftsoons,
eftsoons . . .

Over the hills is okey-doke,
the moon is strawberry pie

TO SETH BUNNEL

CRO-MAGNON SWIRLS THICKLY IN YOUR BLOOD
SWELLING IN A MULTITUDINOUS MIME

of
Being

not just big brain
but the faraway changing

to
atoms of consciousness
like a king snake slung over an antler

engorging his prey
is far older
than Christmas

will ever be

is mammal real energy
IN
YOU

is the place
to perceive your
Father

SPONTANEOUS POEM, MORNING AFTER READING *WHEN I WAS A POET*
for David Meltzer

"I AM THE FULL GROWN OLD MAN HERE
with a hat and boots"
and you are the ancient child growing shoots
of inspiration and genius, each one with multiple buds,
sometimes
drinking sap from the edge of adventures
we had together. Climbing the hill
over and up the trolley tracks in the city
of wind and fog and nerve-jiggling youth.
To confront the tucked-in and grumbly gang
who disliked the delight you carried
in your energy and overflowing fountain.
Now we're at the top of Nob Hill mountain
and it keeps on going, leaving dreams in our sleep.
Pleasures and tortures and friends left behind
or leaping over the stream,
changing shapes around us — sometimes
a shimmer of dust in a pillow's attic,
sometimes a living statue of gold and ivory
as precious as old flesh
AND STUFFED WITH THE AGONY
of waking to sleep again. Taking it slow
in the white-whiskered mirror
reflecting your new love poised in the steam
BEHIND YOU
leaning into the present future.
There's no one like you in the old movies
not Bogart, Chaplin, Lon Chaney,
in the charnel houses to-be of our bop.

No beginning and no stop
JUST THE PROPORTIONLESSNESS
fomenting itself
in every corner or contour of the moment.
We are always there in no present at all.
So we turn back from the peak
and walk into Limbo and Hades
then *zut presto,* we pop out in Paradiso
surrounded by cliff tops of choiring angels
painting our faces on nothingness
with swooping maneuvers
directed by Raphael.

JOANNE KYGER
for Donald Guravich

      YOU ARE THE BLITHE BEAR
  BURSTING THROUGH THE BACK WALL
        to nuzzle the hummingbird

         while Green Tara
           washes
            toes
          that know

        INDIAN SNOWS
       and swarms
          of
Mexican Siestas with Donald.

   These matter in samsara
  like a pink-tinted brooch
     of fossil ivory
  when lights go out
    in the plastic mall
   and the show
      closes

Please plant your foot in the Gate
        so I can slip through after you.

BLAKE FLAKES

1.

STEPPING DOWN
FROM HER SOFT CUBIST CHRYSALIS
the Princess
places her foot
on the naked sleeper.

2.

in the furnace

THE BLUE-BLACK IMP
COVERS HIS EARS

peering down
into
the poet's face.

3.

THE PLUMP NAKED
MANCHILD
pisses on the tusked ogress
in
her cloud of rose petals.

PLUMED STONES

(BLACK AND WHITE WITH RED VEINS)
what am I
BUT A PLUMED
s
t
o
n
e
?
AN APPEARANCE OF MATTER
dreaming antennae and senses
REAL AS TIME AND SMOKE
a serious joke
played on myself
BY MY LOVE
O
F
LIVING

PEEP

>   ALIVE FOR TEN
>   TRILLION
>   YEARS
>   each
>   NEURON
>   a
>   COSMOGENY
>   of plum petals,
>   a drowned aquarium
>   filled with deserts,
>   and carvings
>   of
>   JOY
>
>   assembled from scraps
>
>   of mothers
>   and fathers
>
>   WANTED OR NOT,
>
>   OWNING
>
>   it
>
>   ALL
>
>   raw as the peep of a quail
>
>   or a mastodon charging a lion

DREAM DEEP

GREATNESS IS WHAT WE ASSUME
putting on robes
to

find
we are
already there
or
not

When
dreams
are
deep
and complex

they
are
us

HIGH

ANCIENT ANAXAGORAS
in a fragment said
volatility of the sensorium
is
blunted
by
BEING
— whatever that means —

I

am matter
pulling myself into awakening

I

AM SOUL

ASCENDED

THRICE BLESSED

        HERMES TRISMEGISTUS LEAD
                   ME
          WHERE YOU WOULD
           BE SURE MY SOUL
               is   true
             and my heart
                  is
              understood

SHAKESPEARE'S ROSE

OH PLAIN GLAMOROUS ROSE, I LOVE YOUR OPEN FACE.
YOU SMILE WITH YOUR SEX AT THE SKY.
Milky rose with five white petals
and delicate stamens, where sometimes
the tiny flies and gnats do play.

Crippled rose, rose without scent,
you have no odor,
Shakespeare called you a canker rose
an invalid, a dog rose.
Dear to my heart, opening your sex
to the black bee and the floating hawk

passing beneath the clouds
in the sky.

We
shall
all
pass
and leave no memory.

— And your sweet sister blooms
there
in the clutch.
(how comforting)
Everything needs
the glory of leaves
rich green leaves
and tiny thorns

leaving a memory in the eye
of my thumb

FORGIVENESS PLEASE

      THIS IS ENDLESS AS THE BEGINNING
       of grandiosity shielding the FINITE.
     FALCON-PINIONED GRIFFONS PLOD
         through rose-scented strata
            of nacreous dust

        and the molecular aroma
          of plastic seat covers
         and passing presence
               of
           artificial foods
            and ersatz
                l
                i
                q
                u
                i
                d
                s

          shaped in odd bottles
     to perhaps amuse the fingertips

             WHAT MORE

               do I ask

                 but

         steaming red lobster

whose ancientness dies

for my

pleasure

THE FRANCESCO CLEMENTE POEM

THE BEYOND-COMPREHENSION DETAIL
of superb near-microscopic
pattern and creatures
in the sensual and shocking
SENSUALISMIC
WATERCOLORS

HANG

IN

MY

MIND

like rainbow spume

over wave cliff crash
changing emotions of colors
A
S
encampment palettes of

IMPOSSIBLE ROSINESS,

found only in the odor of new-opened rose,

BECOMES COLOR

by
BLUE
of too-close clouds

GO OUT

></p>

    GO OUT, TINY LONG-LEGGED BEING
OF BLACK GRACE — SLINK AND SPEED
in dewy Autumn grass
with the chipmunks.
Concord's Best Western Motel
is not
your home.
Enjoy this riparian stream.
Walden Pond is too far away
for a
shining cricket.

Watch out
for the Blue Jay!

QUANTUM

              INTELLIGENCES OF MEAT
        FREE TRUTH WITH THEIR BLINDNESS
           opening to the ninety-seven senses
            in the heartfelt nearness and dearness
             and distances of a galactic flood
                of qualia which they shape.
                         THIS
                          IS
                       ALMOST
                      THE TRUTH.

                BUT THIS IS ALL JOY
                          OF
                        BEING
              it says this in capital letters.
              But it is not the voluptuous
                      consciousness
                 of elephants, killer whales,
                   and caterpillars . . .

         but a quantum of endlessness
         that is never felt nor reasoned.

EVIDENCE

THE PRESENCE OF A LAUGH
is a cave lined with pictures
and the smell of rosemary and the call
of a redtail hawk.
An old friend — dead now — shoots up ritalin
SECRETLY
and
I
breathe and walk
the green alley by the canyon.
His mind bursts with it all
into a vision
BLACK
as some Satan's
boot polish.
I hold the evidence.

• • •

LIQUID MERCURY IN THE PALM
of my hand
is a presence.
A
BOY
peering through his semen
at the fortune told
beneath it
in a forest of lines
of pink uncallused stratagems.

. . .

A VULTURE FLIES OVER THE EDGE
of the pine
into an ancient sonata
NOT HIP HOP
or pig-eyed blond billionaires
wanting to be Caligula
or fart jokes from classic antiquity

here is
a
Mobius strip
of
stunned clowns

EVERPRESENT

DAZED WITH THE FANTASY
of scents of molecules, atoms, particles,
superstrings, touches of space,
energy, matter, gravity
— stuff clutching with bonds

Z
I
P
P
E
D

into me,
baby me,

ancient me.

My gorgeous lover
dancing naked and high stepping

dancing to Jeff Beck on guitar.

IS
THIS

A
SPARK

IN EVERPRESENCE

like a giant dolphin

— or is it the music?

TWITTER-IN-CHIEF

MAMMAL MATTERS ARE THE SPONTANEOUS
CHATTER
that floats on a sea of compassion
and not the clatter of madmen
on TV and in the papers.
—The
inflation
and
RAPE
OF CONSCIOUSNESS

is
also
a mammal matter

and real
as lightning and perfume
in the void

and plain
as a plan by Hitler

and the cold grin of a lizard

A CLIMB

    FROM THE NON-BEGINNING OF THE WAVE
            to its endlessness,
        is somewhere where we are,
        and there is monstrous fear
           of death and birth
      that have gathered the earth
          which attracts us

        — these ideas are as real
          as everything else

        — with no Von Humboldt
             BUT ME
      to explore and to measure . . .

FOR STEFANO SCODANIBBIO

STEFANO,
WE ARE HERE, TADPOLES BREATHING, HERE

THE SUN,

the sun and its light.
Seen
FROM
BELOW
we dark stars
W
R
I
T
H
E
with joy,
gnawing
THE ALGAE OF LIFE
and swirling
in
the
freedom
of our swarm
not prepared
to live or die.

It is all dances
AND
LOVE
among stream plants

WE

ARE FREE

in this liberty

ALIVE AS CUPIDS
for Jane

        THE BASEMENT IS MEAT,
          flowings of energy
          through the system,
        NEVER A RAIN BARREL
          always a fountain
            of stars
             born
        of protein to cytoplasm.
      Before there was a dreaming
           NEURON
         to invent existence.
       A romance is dissolved
      by psychic clarity and thus
            HELL
             is
          birthed
   and we are at the beginning

            one
           more
            time

    we must step outside
  the words that handcuff us
    and live as angels
      and cupids
      in new music

I adore love the dry strong feeling
of your fingers
and the tenderness
that is their tendons and muscles

NEVER
LEAVE
ME

you are always gorgeous

SMOKE IN A HAILSTORM

I WOULD BE STRONG — BUT BEING IMMERSED
IN FLESH TAKES THE EDGE OFF
(it is me) and I am here in bio-romantic
CONFUSION LIKE A SCROLL
OF BRILLIANT SLASHES
pretending to be color of Colorado storms

mammal still
still a mammal

FLASHES

OF SORROW CONFUSION CONTRITION
ambition and hunger and sentiment
SADLY AND PROUDLY SENTIENT

trying to cut through a mystery

nobody there
in the spark I disappear

smoke
in
a
hailstorm

Thinking flesh maybe

HOODOO

NO   NO   NO

NO

NO

YOU ARE STRUGGLING TO MAKE

YOUR SKIN
a shrine for demons
like the walls of the coffee shops
brasseries
and half-lit toilets

YOU WILL SUCCEED
and be one more superstitious hoodoo,
grinning, making maps of babbling honesty.
A television screen at last

— a naked success among billions

RAIN ON ORANGE

I AM WHAT I HAVE
THE NERVE TO BE

A HUGE SUCCESS
HIDING IN MEAT.
MAMMAL SHIVERING IN RAIN.
Alarms blast on.
A lion's *Grahhhr* and a hummingbird necklace
on an island where creatures tremble
with superstitions and delighted awe,
holding out skull cups
for a fill of Arab blood
And they stand to their knees
in piss flooding their legs,
between war cries.

WHILE
DARKNESS
WAVE-LAPS AGAINST MOTHERS
and children,

and the intelligent microbial
ocean smiles on

Soft rain on nasturtiums

Amidst electronics

THE RAINY DECK

Inner life of a microbe is so huge that it is minutest particles of nothingness and proportionless-ness

ALL THE WAY
BACK
AND FORWARD
IN MULTI-GLOBAL
DIMENSIONS
AND
DIRECTIONS

not
writhing
but

WITH THE SMILE
and torture
I know.

light in the Junco's eye
gleaning seeds
from the rainy deck
among
fellows

THALASSA

AFTER EATING PEYOTE BUTTONS
IN YOUNG MANHOOD,
there was an heroic struggle to bring
warmth and romance into the COLD
FLAMING
CLARITY
BEYOND
ANIMAL TOUCH
the stark
unreachable . . .

Now
this

all intermixed

like the genetic biome
of the deep ocean

thalassa   thalassa

THE ASHRAF FAYAHD POEM

Big Moslem Souls,
Ashraf Fayahd
is one of you

Mercy, open your Mercy
your Justice
your Great Heartedness

Ashraf Fayahd
is one of you,
Big Moslem Souls

He is a proud figure
for your Mercy,
your Justice,

your Great Heartedness.
Your kindness is the golden flower
to save him

Open your Great Heartedness,
his pride is your pride
bent by spirit,

bent by spirit,
your Great Heartedness
will save him to be,

will save Ashraf Fayahd
to be . . . the child of your
kind, proud Justice.

The poets of the centuries
the Proud and the Modest
entreat Big Moslem Souls

All ask you for Mercy, Justice,
Kindness, for Ashraf Fayahd
Let your justice smile upon

this poet
as a Kind Heart
of a Big Moslem Soul

ANTELOPE BREATH

THE FATE OF A PHOTON
is the numbness
in wrinkled fingertips
and splitting of teeth roots
AS
SCULPTURAL
ACTS
of the body of Phidias
disappearing through a boson
spraying
a
trillion

BEGININGLESS

STATES

TO
INSPIRE

a
photon.

An antelope's breath
scented with wet grass
on
a
taut drumhead.

NITROUS OXIDE HIGH
for Mark Kay

                    M
                    E
                    E
                    R
                    K
                    A
                    T,

Meerkat I, I came and conquered
beetle grubs
&
GODS OF OVERPOPULATION
with Beethoven sonatas
and childhood memories
of sea and beach scent
strawberry, mint,
and turtle breath
in concrete ponds
and
GRANDPA'S EYES
like stones of love

all
of

THIS
WITHOUT PROPORTION

the real point
IN SUBSTANCE

of an imaginary neuron
walking like
a
standing angel
B
E
I
N
G
a child of Shelley
smiling

! !
!

SPREADING PETALS

THE BABY PLUM BLOSSOM OPENS ITS FLOWER
saying, "Dear World, please
do not fade."
YOU ARE MY SWEET MY LOVELY MAID
kissing the world with your lynx-blue eyes
under the *Ragnarok* skies
of pink and blue and salmon and sienna.
(Sometimes in stripes
and often in chunks)
Only sometimes I am afraid
of your nine-tailed rage.
And I adore your outrageous heels
and ankles
lovely as the fruit tree flower
I imagine growing over our bower
where we sniff the lemon opening.
I can barbecue a turkey leg
or poach an egg or create oatmeal
or you can drive us to
The New Gold Medal
for mixed Fun
or slices of pork
anything you desire will work
for me.
Valentines Day is a special one
for Cupid and his Venus.
Hey, we could have congee
at the Lin Jia
A
N
D

mostly remember we are free
to do what we please
laughing and making our bounds

while I LOVE your breasts and kiss
your butt
and other numerous places.

MMMmmmmmmMM

•

THE BABY PLUM BLOSSOMS OPEN THEIR FLOWER
and say,
"Dear World, please do not fade.
The stars are made two hundred billion light years away
to crush in black holes that swirl
like protein and particles of light
morphing into sight
and we are here to rejoice
This petal-spreading and waft
of soft scent is our voice
to plead, please do not fade
till we are gone.

LIGHT   LIGHT   LIGHT
for Richard Olafson

PROTEAN LIFE IS THE GIFT OF MEAT

PROTEIN IS THE SUBSTRATE EMBRACING THE MOLECULE
charged with light
((PROTEAN LIFE IS THE GIFT OF MEAT))

Protein is the substrate embracing a molecule
charged with light.
Light shape-changes the subsrate in a snap.

SPANGLING MOLECULE AND PROTEIN
WRESTLE WITH NON-MEASURABLE ENERGY

AND
vision
(SEEING)
is
birthed

(In the exuberance
imagining giving presence
for
light
and
dark

(SPACE OCEANS OF MATTER AND PHOTONS
breeding flesh for the taste of stars
and apricots

no time no (NEVER) space ever. Not even a body,
no spirit,
everything present as
a
great
HAIKU

What is spirit

is light in my eyes.

*

A trillionic rare angel
trembling and seeing the beginingless

NOVEMBER VALENTINE

INTIMATE SPOTS ARE QUASARS, BOSONS,
the littoral, your armpit and face,
(ready to soon wither),
and the bright reach (stretch) of your eyes.
Your little finger
MOVES ME

more than any moon anywhere
I
LOVE
YOU
and the flow of silken sparks
as you stride across the lobby.
Our days and un-walled moments,
like true poems, are in every dimension
WHERE I
FIND
YOU.
Like Emily Dickinson you
are naked elegance
and I am Thelonius Monk
playing this keyboard
for childhood's ears
NO
ONE
WILL EVER
know.

•

You are the queen of goddesses
and I am your swordsman.
We are hummingbirds in the oak tree.

DETAILS

LET OUR LIVES FALL APART LIKE A TRUE POEM
but we will not be parted
all time is our hour as Dogen
HINTED.
Why else are we here
in the shadow of fear
and hunger and meatly pleasure?
WE ARE THE TREASURE,
the treasures, at the heart of the ivory
universe
in the midst of graffiti trucks and persimmon trees
and dark and light matter,
we are here to be everywhere
caught in scattering
I name it a valentine
holding obsidian mirrors
reflecting
the past back and to the sides
of old toys
and contained tears.
Everything of us is the Messiah.

FA T'SANG

WE ARE THE NEAR EDGE OF THE MOMENT
constructing ourselves as One.
Fa T'sang lectured that any part of the Golden Lion
IS
the Golden Lion even a thought
of that ornament is the thing
and the nothing.
It is less than clear and more
than solid. November valentines
are that. Schrödinger and Whitehead
almost express it but none of it
as active as a higher cell
and colliding galaxies. All bringing
star walls into being or not. No ambivalence.
The Troubador poets sometimes sing it
in the mask of romance.
There are hummingbirds in the oak tree
flying between
branches
in
the
fog.

TINY NAILS

LIKE THE REFLECTION OF A BABY CHICK'S
FOOT on black marble
and then her beak and down seen
against night sky,
her glittering eye
gives the lie
shows the falsity of any concept of proportion.
The new Being hides no distortion
IS THE FLOW
of the randomness of the milieu
shaping life like the fusion
of figure and ground
— or normal words
scatting into irresponsible rhyme
and the nobility
of your queenly face
looking at me like I am the patriarch
of a cadre of fools.
And why not, I think to myself,
why not?
THERE'S A PECK
AND A SCRATCH
of sharp tiny nails!

NO SAVIOR

YOU ARE NOT GOING TO DIE HERE
HAVE NO FEAR
OR HOPE. Everywhere is nowhere
You are not going to die here
NOWHERE IS ALIVE
in the dark in neon and headlights
smothering the shine of stars in the deep
or in the shallows. You are not
going to die here. Matter is in the voice
of nothing. Matter *is* the voice
of nothing — all ears, eyes, and nose.
There's no lord for animals
or the souls they make themselves.

ONE LIFE TO LIVE through creates a time
love   life   time

use the beginningless
unending

There is no vale but this.

there is no other vale

It is gone — it is *mukti* — you are free

we are all — are *mukti* — are free

DECEMBER SEMAPHORE
for Terry and Ann Riley

IN THE PRESENCE OF GENIUS AND CHARM,
nothing right or wrong just a glow
with the taste of winter pear
lighting the temples — and the pleasure
of living in *moksha*. Brought to light
by the red and black depth of the fireplace
and the smile of a grinning new bairn
reaching to tangle her fingers
in a curly white beard
while we speak of music.

VENICE BEACH, AT LAST

WE BELONG IN THE POWER OF MUSIC
Dust storms in the sand and crows
on the boardwalk. Bare legs in the bland
DOMESTICATION.
Paintings of giant ground sloths
smeared on the cliff above the burger shop.
We breathe, we hope. The rope-a-dope
holds us here nestling sneers

IN PUISSANCE

THE
DANCE
IS PROTEINS.

A solid mass creating space in the sound

GALAXIES BURSTING IN FAIRY TALES

IN THE LISTENING.

Scent.   Taste.   Touch.   Smell.

The starting bell.

LUNGOMARE

STARK RAVING REALITY TURNED HELPLESSLY
into matter — to love and to wrestle
the breasts of imagination. Just a chickadee
upside down on the bark
OF A YOUNG PINE
sheltered from the storm

OF

THUNDER

AND

LIGHTNING

in

a

moment

of silvery flood

with the beach mountains

and the opening and closing

curtains of clouds in the crash
and clack of the silence
and the fresh clear smell

GREETING

    MORTALITY IS BEAUTY   THE BEAST SPIRIT
LIVES FOREVER
IN FIGURES OF FLESH
that may not know their inhabitants.
Our shapes are meeting as we always greet another.
Love invented by nights on horseback
and infinite senses in the saddle
— this myriad trail
IN
ALL DIMENSIONS.

SACRED FIGURES
aglomerations
of matter and bacteria.
LORD BYRON DRUNK IN HIS COMEDY
OF DIVINITY.
Cold littoral divides toes and surge.
SWIRLS
OF
STAR DUST

right
here
!

MESEMBRYANTHEMUMS

MESEMBRYANTHEMUMS

A
M
O
N
G

thistles

— white pink yellow —
shivering petals
praising sunlight

Step quickly

OH GULLS

and
beware
of white-faced
sea

O
T
T
E
R
S

FOR AMY

SLEEPING WHITE-HEAD OTTERS
BACKFLOAT
IN AND OUT
O
F
the pod

like a spirit
of
ANARCHY

May I be so blithe
as missing
memory returns.

Recollecting
"NEZAHUALCOYOTL"
just as
my search begins.

One bumps into another
They snarl and slap
and smile

NEURONS
LIGHTING
the
waves

WRINKLES AND SCARS

WRINKLES AND SCARS
MEDALLIONS
OF
AGE,

I

A

M

SOON TO BE
FIBROUS TISSUE
on bare feet.
Pleased
without rage
a calendar in a cage

WRINKLES OF EYE BAGS
will
mask the face.

I'll rob banks
—A Dillinger
and a Clyde
with my booful
AMY

WHARF PILINGS

        MILK WHITE
      FORESTS OF BOUQUETS:

          MILK
           W
           H
           I
           T
           E

    sea anemones
      flourishing.

     Fish flutter

   small rays skim

  through the cosmos

of phytoplankton and zooplankton

      by wharf
      pilings —

SKELETON KEY

ARTHUR DOVE LIVES ON
our wall at Lighthouse Lodge

A *GRANDMA COLLAGE*
O
F
BEACH SCATTERINGS
colorful prints of top side and bottom
of large snail
by a large snail shell
seven pieces of beach debris
skinny large white starfish
wooden bingo coins
crusted white turtle stone
dark seaweed frond in tree pattern
partly legible poem
by Nezahualcoyotl.

That's it
LIVE ON ARTHUR
V
I
V
A
!!!

— OOOPS, a white bleached
periwinkle shell!

UH-OH...!
— A SKELETON KEY

LATE WINTER

                COYOTE
                    on
                  back
                  yard
                  deer
                  trail

                  RAIN
                washes
                    out
                    toad
                  stools

WITH SIMONE FATTAL AT THE HOCKNEY SHOW

— BEWILDERING —

AN ACT OF NATURE

DON'T LOSE
yourself

A
JEWELED SUPERCAVERN
inside a continent-sized Mont Blanc
changing radiances of fabulosities

not
a
MAMMAL
IN
SITE.

GAY PORTRAITS
of mock-straights

Wear your sunglasses!

YES

                YES
    THERE IS NO SYMMETRY BUT
poetry, biology, imagination, and science
      the rest, if any, is simple
    as the eyelashes of Blake blinking
    above his watercolors for Dante

— Beatrice standing thinly veiled on the chariot
       drawn by the sturdy griffon
or the monster Fraud hovering with tender smile
      as he drops into Malebolge
  ferrying the poets, as Virgil commands.
Carpe noctem, seize the night and winter.
      Let things standing together
    be a monument to their absence.
      UNCERTAINTY IS PLAY

AND THE HEART POURS FORTH FROM CHILDHOOD

    — The first blueblack jay ever seen
      in a bouquet of wet trees . . .
    The turtle sleeping at pond's edge
  under the dahlias and the cherry tree
    with lumps of sap on the trunk . . .

My Grandfather sniffing snuff and sneezing

    IT'S ALL THE PARK
          OF
         OLD
         AGE
  on the first day of Spring.

JOKO DAVE HASELWOOD

SOMEWHERE A PLUM IS RIPE
lifting in thunderous rain
through black roots.
Somewhere we all die
in
our
LIVING
from
ear lobes
to toes in the earth.
Like stars and mitochondria
with no future or past
to present.

SPIRIT NEURONS
A CROW BAR

SPIRIT-NEURONS
make the stream of words
a thousand times more lovely.
It is inside-out that these things
SHOULD
BE
in childhood
when I terrorized black ants' nests.
Life is there like cavernous kisses
carved from scarlet celluloid.

"Touch me.

Let me feel
I'm
still alive
in
you."

But I can only touch me
through your hands!
And there are many-colored clouds
around this.

WE
UNDERSTAND
that we are straw
made of lightning
with life-strands reaching

into
realms
beyond
comprehension;
for understanding is a prank

and
THIS MIGHT BE A CROW BAR!

DYING IS NOTHINGNESS

1.

IT MAY BE THE WAY OF ALL FLESH
to sense backward through itself:
(ORGANS, TISSUES AND SYSTEMS
OF DANCING LOVERS
MAKING CELLS)

and also to see the sides and front through
star banks
in the eyes of a sparrow.

2.

BEING BORN IS NOTHINGNESS
DYING IS NOTHINGNESS
Grandpa and Mama are nothingness
and I am here with
ALL LIVES
I
N
VENTING

a love
HALF FREE

Coming into being is matter
passing through is not matter;

in the black deeps
light eats light,
shitting coal.

THE MASK OF GRAMMAR

THE MASK OF GRAMMAR AND SOCIAL EXACTNESS
IS NOT A VASE TO HOLD THE SHOOTS
of budding (luxuriantly fragranced) basil. The humming bird
speeds by the window
and her mask and consciousness are the same
BUT
I
can emancipate myself from even
near freedom
by being the dumb bunny I am
AND I AM
BECOMING
an athlete of openness,
a lover of the elephant-eared
translucent octopus (newly discovered)
floating in the ocean's Hadal depths,
or your true love in naked dreams
claiming THIS is what truly matters.

What is the material gate,
when the gate is all realms AT ONCE?

•

(For the shop keepers)

In the dark, and lighted, front yard
of the shop in the rain
on the busy street, sleek burly
bulks of raccoons watch us fearlessly
and pick with dainty nails among the fallen leaves.

ESSAY ON THE MEDIA (1971)
for Carl Landauer

1. GAMES SUCK.

2. GAMESMANSHIP BECOMES NEOPLATONIC.

3. THE HUMAN PERSONALITY BECOMES ONE WITH THE HUMANISTIC PUBLIC FIGURE.

4. THERE ARE NOT ENOUGH MAMMAL SEARCHLIGHTS TURNED ON THE RUBBLE.

5. EVERYONE INTERVIEWS THEMSELVES WHILE THEY ARE LEAPING WITH ECSTASY OR DYING THEIR CRISIS.

6. THERE ARE TOO FEW INTENTIONAL SPIRITUAL DE-CONDITIONINGS.

7. THE CONDITIONED REFLEX IS ADAPTABLE TO ALTERNATIVE NEOPLATONISMS.

8. IDEALISTIC POSTURING IS NOT INDIVIDUATION.

9. THERE ARE MANY MORE MOSESES THAN THERE ARE MOUNTAINS.

10. MANY MOSESES SCRAMBLING FOR MOUNTAINS.

11. THE MEDIA IS THE MOUNTAIN.

12. NEOPLATONISM IS THE TERRITORY.

13. RHETORIC IS THE EVANGELISM.

14. TECHNOLOGY IS THE BACKGROUND.

15. MADNESS IS FEEDBACK FROM THE BACKGROUND.

16. NEOPLATONIC EXHORTATIONS ARE THE MANIFESTATION.

17. TRIPPING.

18. HOLOCENE CONDITIONINGS.

19. THE CANARY HAS SWALLOWED THE CAT.

20. THE CAT LIKES IT.

21. THE CANARY RADIATES NEOPLATONISMS.

22. THE CANARY CANNOT SEE THE QUESTION MARK OVER HIS HEAD.

23. THE CANARY HEARS HIMSELF WARBLING HARTZ MOUNTAIN MELODIES.

24. THE CAT IS PURRING.

25. MACHINES ARE BUILDING A MACHINE FOR THE CANARY.

26. THERE WILL BE AN ELECTRONIC CANARY — WITH NO CAT IN HIM.

27. GAMES KEEP THE PLAYERS VERY BUSY.

28. DID.

29. YOU.

30. KNOW.

31. THAT.

32. ?

RED CAGES

    THIS
    IS
    THE
    WAR

    OF
    BEING

    A
    BODY

    IT
    IS
    THE
    BODY
    being
     a
    war

this is the war of being a body
this is the war of being a body
it is the body being a war
  and I surrender

    AND

    I
    CEASE

  the conflict

and I surrender

    AND

    I
   CEASE

  the conflict

 but the waves do not stop
     but the waves do not stop
though I am calm
   and quiet

and the waves are fields
  and the fields are a war
and the war is a path
  and the path is smooth
    as the muscles knotted in the war
  of the child's head thrown back

gasping,   after the screaming:

      "I WANT MY MOTHER"

       WHERE
       THE
       DARK
      SHADOWS
       ARE

WHERE THE SUNSHINE
IS

Where the car starts in the fog
    where the fox barks
  Where oil drips over the lip
      of the curb

Where the body is thrown fifteen feet
      by the crash of the taxi
      in the night street
      in front of the crumbling hotel

it is the war of being a body
It is the war of being a body
it is the body of being a war

    and I surrender

    TO
    THE
    DEEP
    THINGS

    TO
    THE
    DEEP
    THINGS

    WAY BACK IN THERE

AND THERE IS NO END TO THE DEPTH
      THAT THEY COME FROM

THAT IS MY SOUL OUT THERE

THAT IS MY SOUL OUT THERE

     where
      the
       war
  is the path of my body

         •

      SOME

       WHERE

        IN

       THE

      CAVE

       OF

        A

     CLOUD

    I

    LAUGH

    AT THE CIRCUS

      at the Red Cages

      at the ponies

      at the shoes of the clowns

I
AM
MY
BODY

  BEING THE WAR

    of the Circus

    in the cave of the cloud

while the tv blares in the stars
      the mosquito buzzes
the birds' songs are roars

    and I surrender

to the buzz of mosquitoes
and the clouds of the stars
in the war of the circus

AS
I
WALK
THROUGH
THE
BUTTERMILK
SMELL
OF
RHODODENDRONS

I don't want to be strange
   this is me
I don't want to be strange
   this is me
shallow as a small stream
that trickles
through the waves
where the birds and the buildings

roar
it is the body being a war
where the soul feasts
on all souls

and the children die
in the mortar concussions

      I
      WILL

NOT
EAT

THE
MEAT

that is mine
OR THE SOUL
that I grow

in April

I DON'T WANT TO BE STRANGE
this is me

in the war of the waves

of the meat

I surrender

I
CEASE

TO
BE

the roar of the war

in the roaring war

of the waves
that is me

and I laugh at the floppy shoes
of the clowns
and the groans of the ponies
hit by the taxis

AND
THE
RED
CAGES

mired in the stream
where
the fox barks
at the pictures reflected
in the drip of the oil

I surrender
  I
    CEASE

but the waves do not stop
but the waves do not stop
but the waves do not stop

though I am calm and quiet
though I am calm and quiet
   and the waves are fields
   and the fields are a war
   though I am calm and quiet
   as a cricket being a star
      in the roar

BOULDER HILL
for Amy

SURE, YEAH, THIS IS MINE, / THIS IS MY INTERIOR
where the dark matters lie as I come to the light
of the setting sun where the boulders stand
where we stop by the dusty path, hand in hand,
    and peer where the mating oak moths fly
      like ghost silhouettes in the gloaming sky
        making patterns
                      and flights
      in the green spiky leaves.
        YOU & I
      are the sheaves
        of this Something Else
          that crawled
          and danced
           and sang
           and spun
            till
        that ancient thought
          called Matter
      stood on the toes that it made
      and pushed us out,
    trembling, scared, hungry, unafraid,
    in a twisting mass of gleaming guts
      and poetry and silence and listening
  and sniffing and snuffing and chatter
          AND
           WE
          WATCH
        just this once
         in wonder
        of dreamy awe

as these moths flatter
the nerves that reach from our eyes
to our brains and our shoulders and fingers
AND
NOW
out of nowhere
we've stepped into
YOUR INTERIOR
as it overlaps
and pours like a stream
in-
to
mine
and we laugh out loud
with pleasure
as our stomachs chill
with primordial fear
at the wide-mouthed, fangy, pink hiss
of the mottled gopher snake
who lies on the crevice in her boulder,
as she hides her fright
of us
with brave aggression.
It is our obsession
to be as entwined
as the atoms
in a molecule
of
DNA
and our souls cross
one another

    like chakras where the nerve tubes pass
on the body of the goddess Kundalini.

Look, the small plane, rattling over,
    shakes the petals of the mariposa lily
where the black beetle stands
              with his butt in the air.
Soon the salamander will
          come out for a stroll
and to enlighten our stare
he'll leave the prints
of his feet and tail in the dust
and amphibian dreams in the air.

ALSO BY MICHAEL MCCLURE

POETRY

Passage
Hymns to St. Geryon and Other Poems
Dark Brown
Ghost Tantras
The New Book/A Book of Torture
Dark Brown and *Hymns to St. Geryon*
Poisoned Wheat
Little Odes
Star
Rare Angel
September Blackberries
Jaguar Skies
Antechamber
Fragments of Perseus
Selected Poems
Rebel Lions
Simple Eyes
Three Poems: Dolphin Skull, Rare Angel, and Dark Brown
Huge Dreams: San Francisco and Beat Poems
Touching the Edge: Dharma Devotions from the Hummingbird Sangha
Rain Mirror
Plum Stones: Cartoons of No Heaven
Mysteriosos and Other Poems
Of Indigo and Saffron: New and Selected Poems
Mephistos & Other Poems

PLAYS

The Blossom; or Billy the Kid
The Beard
The Mammals
Gargoyle Cartoons
Gorf, or Gorf and the Blind Dyke
The Grabbing of the Fairy
Josephine: The Mouse Singer
The Beard & VKTMS: Two Plays

ESSAYS, INTERVIEWS, BIOGRAPHY

Meat Science Essays
Wolf Net
Freewheelin Frank: Secretary of the Angels, as Told to Michael McClure
Scratching the Beat Surface: Essays on New Vision from Blake to Kerouac
Specks
Francesco Clemente: Testa Coda
Lighting the Corners: On Art, Nature, and the Visionary, Essays and Interviews

NOVELS

The Mad Cub
The Adept

COLLABORATIONS

"Mercedes Benz," with Janis Joplin
Mandala Book, with Bruce Conner
The Adventures of a Novel, with Bruce Conner
Lie, Stand, Sit, Be Still, with Robert Graham
The Boobus and the Bunnyduck, with Jess Collins
Deer Boy, with Hung Liu

FILMS, CDS, AND DVDS

Love Lion, with Ray Manzarek
The Third Mind, with Ray Manzarek
There's a Word, with Ray Manzarek
I Like Your Eyes Liberty, with Terry Riley
Rock Drill
Abstract Alchemist
Rebel Roar
Touching the Edge

DOCUMENTARIES

The Maze
September Blackberries

Michael McClure is an award-winning American poet, playwright, songwriter, and novelist. A key figure of the Beat Generation, McClure is immortalized as Pat McLear in Jack Kerouac's novels *The Dharma Bums* and *Big Sur*. He also participated in the '60s counterculture alongside musicians like Janis Joplin and Jim Morrison. McClure remains active as a poet, essayist, and playwright, and lives with his wife, Amy, in the San Francisco Bay area.

www.ingramcontent.com/pod-product-compliance
Lightning Source LLC
Chambersburg PA
CBHW060458080526
44584CB00015B/1470